photoword book

Fruit

Camilla Lloyd

WAYLAND

zwijsen
bdyslexie font
is the typeface used in this book

First published in 2014 by Wayland
Copyright © Wayland 2014

Wayland
338 Euston Road
London NW1 3BH

Wayland Australia
Level 17/207 Kent Street
Sydney, NSW 2000

Editor: Elizabeth Brent
Designer: Amy McSimpson

Dewey number: 428.1-dc23

ISBN   978 0 7502 8294 9
eBook ISBN   978 0 7502 8524 7

Printed in China

10 9 8 7 6 5 4 3 2 1

Picture acknowledgements: All images,
including the cover image, courtesy of
Shutterstock.com, except: p4–5 © Cristian
Baitg/iStockPhoto, p6 © NoDerog/iStockPhoto,
p12 © Jasmina007/iStockPhoto

The website addresses (URLs) included in this book
were valid at the time of going to press. However,
it is possible that contents or addresses may
change following the publication of this book.
No responsibility for any such changes can be
accepted by either the author or the Publisher.

Wayland is a division of Hachette Children's Books,
an Hachette UK company.
www.hachette.co.uk

Contents

fruit

There are lots of different types of fruit.

Eating **fruit** is very good for you.

apples

These are apples.

6

Apples are
crunchy!

7

peaches

This is a
peach.

8

Peaches have a furry skin.

9

oranges

These are **oranges**.

You can **squeeze** oranges to make orange juice.

strawberries

These are **strawberries**

Strawberries grow in the **summer**.

pears

These are pears.

Pears grow on trees.

plums

These are plums.

Plums have stones in them.

grapes

These are
grapes.

Grapes can be green or red.

17

kiwis

These are kiwis.

Kiwis have a **scratchy** skin.

18

pineapples

These are pineapples.

Pineapples have a **spiky** skin.

bananas

This is a banana.

You **peel** a banana to eat the fruit.

Picture quiz

Can you find these words in the book?

furry

scratchy

spiky

crunchy

What pages are
they on?

Index quiz

The index is on page 24.
Use the index to answer these questions.

1. Which page shows **plums**?
   What do plums have inside them?

2. Which page shows **strawberries**?
   When do strawberries grow?

3. Which page shows **pears**?
   Where do pears grow?

4. Which page shows **oranges**?
   What can you make with oranges?

Index

Answers

Picture quiz: 'Furry' is on page 9. 'Scratchy' is on page 18. 'Spiky' is on page 19. 'Crunchy' is on page 7.
Index quiz: 1. Page 15, stones; 2. Pages 12 & 13, summer; 3. Page 14, trees; 4. Pages 10 & 11, juice.

24